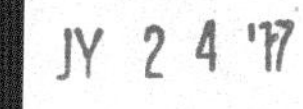

Alexander Graham Bell

by Emily James

CAPSTONE PRESS
a capstone imprint

Barrington Area Library
505 N. Northwest Highway
Barrington, IL 60010
847-382-1300 • balibrary.org

Pebble Plus is published by Capstone Press,
1710 Roe Crest Drive, North Mankato, Minnesota 56003
www.mycapstone.com

Copyright © 2017 by Capstone Press, a Capstone imprint. All rights reserved.
No part of this publication may be reproduced in whole or in part, or stored in a retrieval system, or transmitted in any form or by any means, electronic, mechanical, photocopying, recording, or otherwise, without written permission of the publisher.

Library of Congress Cataloging-in-Publication Data
Names: James, Emily, author.
Title: Alexander Graham Bell / by Emily James.
Description: North Mankato, Minnesota : Capstone Press, a Capstone imprint, [2017] | Series: Pebble plus. Great scientists and inventors | Audience: Ages 4–8. | Audience: K to grade 3. | Includes bibliographical references and index.
Identifiers: LCCN 2016032846 | ISBN 9781515738831 (library binding) | ISBN 9781515738893 (pbk.) | ISBN 9781515739074 (ebook (pdf))
Subjects: LCSH: Bell, Alexander Graham, 1847–1922—Juvenile literature. | Inventors—United States—Biography—Juvenile literature. | Telephone—History—Juvenile literature.
Classification: LCC TK6143.B4 J36 2017 | DDC 621.385/092 [B] —dc23
LC record available at https://lccn.loc.gov/2016032846

Editorial Credits
Jaclyn Jaycox and Michelle Hasselius, editors; Jennifer Bergstrom, designer; Jo Miller, media researcher; Steve Walker, production specialist

Photo Credits
Alamy: Pictorial Press, 17; Getty Images: Archive Photos/Smith Collection/Gado, 7, Bettmann, 13, National Geographic/Dr. Gilbert H. Grosvenor, 15, The LIFE Picture Collection/Mansell/Time Life Pictures, 11; Newscom: Ken Welsh, 19, ZUMA Press/JT Vintage, cover, 1, 21; Science Source, 9; Wikimedia: Kim Traynor, 5

Design Elements: Shutterstock: aliraspberry, Charts and BG, mangpor2004, Ron and Joe, sumkinn, Yurii Andreichyn

Note to Parents and Teachers

The Great Scientists and Inventors set supports national curriculum standards for social studies related to people, places, and culture. This book describes and illustrates the life of Alexander Graham Bell. The images support early readers in understanding the text. The repetition of words and phrases helps early readers learn new words. This book also introduces early readers to subject-specific vocabulary words, which are defined in the Glossary section. Early readers may need assistance to read some words and to use the Table of Contents, Glossary, Read More, Internet Sites, Critical Thinking Using the Common Core, and Index sections of the book.

Printed and bound in China.
PO7886LEOS17

Table of Contents

FAMILY

Alexander Graham Bell was born in Edinburgh, Scotland in 1847. His father was a teacher who taught people how to speak clearly.

Edinburgh, Scotland

Alexander's mother was deaf. But she was a gifted pianist. She taught him how to play the piano. Alexander was good at music and science.

Alexander Graham Bell

Alexander with his mother, father, and brothers in 1870

EARLY YEARS

Alexander was interested in
sound and how it travels.
He also liked to invent things.
Alexander built his first invention
when he was 12 years old.

Alexander at
age 14 or 15

In 1871 Alexander moved to Boston, Massachusetts. He taught deaf students how to communicate. He also experimented with sound.

Alexander and his students at Boston School for the Deaf in 1871

Alexander wanted to learn about electricity. In 1874 he met Tom Watson. Tom knew how electricity worked.

Alexander Graham Bell (left) and Tom Watson

INVENTING THE TELEPHONE

Alexander stopped teaching. He and Tom wanted to invent a machine. They hoped it would send voices from one place to another.

Alexander testing an invention that collects moisture

On March 10, 1876, Alexander
and Tom reached their goal.
They invented the first telephone.
The two men spoke to each
other through the machine.

The first words Alexander said on the telephone were, "Mr. Watson, come here. I want you."

LATER YEARS

Alexander and Tom made their telephone better. Soon it could send voices over many miles. In 1915 they made the first telephone call across the United States.

Alexander at the opening of the long-distance telephone line from New York to Chicago in 1892

Alexander died in 1922 as a respected teacher and inventor. His work had changed the way people communicate with each other.

Alexander in 1920

Glossary

communicate—to pass along thoughts, feelings, or information

deaf—being unable to hear

electricity—a natural force that can be used to make light and heat or to make machines work

experiment—a scientific test to find out how something works

invent—to think up and make something new

pianist—someone who plays the piano

respect—to have a high opinion of someone

Read More

Davis, Lynn. *Alexander Graham Bell.* Amazing Inventors and Innovators. Minneapolis: Abdo Publishing, 2016.

Kramer, Barbara. *Alexander Graham Bell.* National Geographic Kids. Washington, D.C.: National Geographic, 2015.

Lin, Yoming S. *Alexander Graham Bell and the Telephone.* Eureka! New York: PowerKids Press, 2012.

Internet Sites

FactHound offers a safe, fun way to find Internet sites related to this book. All of the sites on FactHound have been researched by our staff.

Here's all you do:

Visit *www.facthound.com*

Type in this code: 9781515738831

Check out projects, games and lots more at
www.capstonekids.com

Critical Thinking Using the Common Core

1. What did Alexander's mother teach him to do when he was a child? (Key Ideas and Details)
2. Alexander liked to invent things. What does "invent" mean? (Craft and Structure)
3. Imagine you are Alexander on March 10, 1876. You are about to make the first telephone call. What would you say? (Integration of Knowledge and Ideas)

Index